Playing with Fire

Playing with
Fire

by
John Weldon
and
James Bjornstad

MOODY PRESS
CHICAGO

Scripture quotations in this book are from the *New American Standard Bible,* © 1960, 1962, 1963, 1968, 1971, 1972, 1973, 1975, and
1977, by The Lockman Foundation, and are used by permission.

Library of Congress Cataloging in Publication Data

Weldon, John.
  Playing with fire.

  Bibliography: p.
  1. Fantasy games—Religious aspects—Christianity.
2. Dungeons and dragons (Game)—Case studies.
I. Bjornstad, James.   II. Title.
GV1202.F35W45 1984   794.2   84-14747
ISBN 0-8024-0425-1 (pbk.)

1 2 3 4 5 6 7 Printing/B + /Year 88 87 86 85 84

Printed in the United States of America

Contents

9 Nov 84

69779

John Weldon wishes to express appreciation to the following for their friendship and kindness:

Bill and Loretta Bowers
Tom and Naomi Brewer
Steve and Susan Clark
Mike Dosh
Phil and Nancy Miller

*   *   *

To Christine, who continually encouraged her father to finish this manuscript, and to Karen, who rose early each morning to "write her own book" while her father wrote his.—James Bjornstad

Introduction

Introduction

Picture yourself in

the cavernous interior of ancient ruins near the city of Welkeep, in the elfin kingdom of Celene. Hunting for treasure are Talmat, an elfin fighter, Bushido, a dwarf cleric, and two humans—Galloway, a thief, and a magician named Citatzner.

They enter a room filled with broken furniture. There is a fine gray dust on the floor, three inches deep. As the four adventurers walk, two imposing creatures swirl up from beneath them.

"They both have swords, they both look nasty, and they're blocking the entrance," says the Dungeon Master.

A few quick thrusts of Talmat's sword reveal the figures from the floor to be harmless dust phantoms. But as they turn a corner, four apelike monsters are charging at the group.

In the ensuing melee, the monsters are subdued and their throats slit. But Galloway has been severely injured. Bushido conjures a healing spell.[1]

Or, picture yourself there when

1. *The Sunday Record,* 8 March 1981.

suddenly all our terrors take form as Greg tells us about a mysterious woman in a white gown. What is she? A vampire? Greg rolls the dice. "She's a chaotic illusion. But she's not a vampire." While we speculate, she attacks like a madwoman. We explode into counterattack, our dice throws telling us how much damage we're doing. We hit her four times, tearing off her arm. Urgrurl slashes her in the abdomen. Wyvark, thrilled to be fighting evil at last, spears her in the head. Greg describes the awesome sight. "She's staggering. It looks like a shimmer spell. She is dissolving into thin air." Will she heal herself and return? As dungeon master, only Greg knows that she is a succubus, that luscious demon of mythology who descends on men when they are asleep in lonely outposts and lures them to sexual intercourse. Greg will bring her back on some other run, perhaps in her male form as an incubus who impregnates women as they sleep.[2]

Contrary to what you might expect, you are not sitting around a campfire on the eve of a full moon, listening to some fascinating (or frightening) medieval tales and monster stories. Nor are you watching a double feature of *The Nightstalker* on television. No, you are not having nightmares, either, from reading too much medieval fantasy and occult literature or watching too many late night horror shows. What you would find yourself in the middle of is some of the fantasy action and adventure of two different sessions of Dungeons and Dragons® (D & D), a fantasy role-playing (FRP) game currently enjoyed by more than three million players.

Why the great interest today in such games as Dungeons and Dragons®, Tunnels and Trolls, Chivalry and Sorcery, RuneQuest®, Arduin Grimoire, Swordbearers, and Demons? There are several factors best understood as part of the effects of a revolution in the way we view the world that help to explain this.

2. Moira Johnston, "It's Only a Game—Or Is It?" *New West,* 25 August 1980, p. 37.

In the early 1950s naturalism was the dominant world view.[3] Along with its accompanying doctrine of rationalism, naturalism not only provided the basic paradigm for perceiving and explaining reality, it also provided the setting in which games were created and fiction and fantasy were written. According to this world view, man is a rational creature. As such, his tendency is to perceive and understand everything from a natural and reasonable perspective.

Naturalism was, however, incapable of providing all man sought for and needed. Although going a long way toward meeting man's need in a variety of areas, it had done so on a purely material, technological level. Once those goals were attained, man, who was dissatisfied with materialistic lifestyles and the answers of a rational and optimistic humanism, was left uncertain about the deeper meaning of life. Though naturalism continues to be a major philosophy, in recent years new world views have emerged to allow for different and greater explanations of reality.

One of the new world views replaced the matter of naturalism with some divine force, power, or consciousness permeating the universe in its entirety. This world view not only radically altered the perception of the world but also established an eclectic world view necessary for intense interest in science fiction and certain fantasy; an inclusion of superbeings and mythological gods; excursions into the magical, the mystical, and the unknown; pursuit of sorcery and spiritualism; and much more. According to this world view, man becomes the prime reality. As such, his tendency is to perceive and understand things in terms of himself. Thus he explores new horizons, chooses those elements that appeal to him, and, in some sense, even creates his own universe around him.

3. The definition of a world view, as used throughout this book, is "a set of presuppositions (or assumptions) which we hold (consciously or subconsciously) about the basic make-up of our world." James Sire, *The Universe Next Door* (Downers Grove, Ill.: Inter-Varsity, 1976), p. 17.

It is this mystical-occult world view that provides, first of all, the "universe" for the current fascination with the mystical, the occult, and the unknown. This is the very setting in which fantasy role-playing games develop their fantasy milieu and in which all the excitement and adventure takes place. Second, it provides the "potential" for man to be "somebody" and the "power" for man to be "greater than he really is." This, of course, may be fulfilled in FRP games where the player can be his character and develop his alter ego, have powers never attainable on earth, "create" his own universe, and so on. As one can easily see, fantasy and FRP games are natural in this world view. (Unfortunately, so also is the occult.)

What about these FRP games? Are they merely games? Can they be separated from their world view? What about the current controversy over these games? How can one discern what is wholesome today from what is not? In the succeeding chapters we will attempt to answer these and other questions and to consider all the evidence regarding FRP games. Join us now as we begin to "examine everything carefully; hold fast to that which is good; abstain from every form of evil" (1 Thessalonians 5:21-22).

It's Merely a Game—
Or Is It?

1

It's Merely a Game— Or Is It?

Fantasy role-playing (FRP) games have been taking the nation by storm since they were first introduced to students on college campuses in 1975. At first these games were little more than an obscure diversion enjoyed by relatively few. Today they have virtually become a national pastime. Beginning with an estimated sales of $150,000 in 1975, sales had skyrocketed to an estimated $150 million in 1982—and sales are still soaring. Although FRP games rank behind their electronic competitors, they have become popular amusement for millions of people.

Interest in playing these games, however, is not the only aspect that has been growing during the past few years. More and more people have become concerned about these games, especially <u>Dungeons and Dragons®, the first and most popular of all FRP games.</u>

Perhaps the earliest public concern was in 1979, when James Dallas Egbert III, an undergraduate student at the University of Michigan and an avid Dungeons and Dragons® player, mysteriously disappeared. There was speculation among his friends and fellow students that his disappearance was associated with some bizarre Dungeons and Dragons® plot. The prevailing theory at that time was that his fantasy world had become more real to him than his everyday world and that he had become disoriented—lost in time and space—moving through a twisted nightmarish dimension like a zombie. The news media picked up on this, and, of course, the reports in newspapers and on radio and television helped to generate concern about this game. Within a month, Egbert was found unharmed in Texas, and there was no apparent connection between his disappearance and Dungeons and Dragons®.

The commotion over Egbert and the resultant national publicity not only created some concern about the game but also massive interest in it. All over the country, people flocked to the stores to buy this game. Stores could not keep up with the demand, and even TSR Hobbies, Inc., the manufacturer, soon completely exhausted its supply. Moira Johnston does not appear to have overstated the significance of Egbert to the escalated interest in the game when she wrote:

> They should raise a foundation to this Egbert kid. Except for the disappearance of that boy and the resulting national exposure, TSR could have remained a steadily growing hobby-game company instead of a skyrocketing one. Even Gygax (the game's inventor) now admits that "ultimately, it was immeasurably helpful to us in name of recognition. We ran out of stock."[1]

One year later Egbert committed suicide. His death sparked new speculations and concerns. However, an investigation of his death and the surrounding circumstances brought forth no conclusive evidence to connect his suicide with Dungeons and Dragons®.

Concern over Egbert was soon forgotten or relegated to the

---

1. Moira Johnston, *New West*, 25 August 1980, p. 37.

past. But it was only a matter of time before other cases of apparent FRP-related problems (suicides, murders, demon possession, overidentification with characters, inability to distinguish between fantasy and reality, etc.) were to emerge.

Consider, for example, the case of Irving Lee Pulling II. Pulling was a very talented sixteen-year-old high school student who, on June 9, 1982, came home from school, went to his room, and committed suicide by shooting himself in the chest with a pistol. It seems that Pulling had a keen interest in science fiction and wars and was an ardent player of Dungeons and Dragons®. It is alleged that a few hours before his suicide Pulling was playing the game with other students at his high school. In the course of events while playing the game, a "curse was placed on him (on his character) by another player." Contending that young people carry their FRP experiences over into real life, his parents believe that this curse disturbed him and placed him under emotional distress, resulting in his suicide later that day. Since Dungeons and Dragons® was allowed to be played as an "organized school activity at the high school," they filed a lawsuit for $1,000,000 in damages and legal expenses against the principal, charging that he, as the chief administrator at the high school, was the one ultimately responsible.[2] The court decided that neither the teacher involved nor the principal were responsible for Pulling's death.

The Pullings subsequently filed a $10 million lawsuit against TSR Hobbies, the manufacturer of D & D. They maintain that their son's suicide was the result of following precise instructions found in D & D materials. They believe their son had concluded that the way to remove the curse placed on him was to offer himself as a human sacrifice. Apparently he had calculated that if this was done by a certain time he would have a 97 percent chance of resurrection.[3]

2. *The Washington Post*, 13 August 1983.
3. "Dungeons and Dragons, Part 2," on "The 700 Club," June 13, 1984.

Or consider the case of the "freeway murders" in southern California in which several people, including children, were murdered as part of what now appears to have been an adventure. Allegedly, one of the young men responsible for these killings was an obsessive player of Dungeons and Dragons®. At the age of 21 he was so preoccupied with this game that it had become his whole life. At times he would play twenty-four hours a day. His room had been made over into a medieval fantasy world. Occasionally he would put on make-up and dress in the attire of his character, the magic user. Finally, his identification with his character apparently became so overwhelming he decided to become a magic user in this world. With the hope of gaining real power, he joined a satanic coven and was initiated into Satanism.

It has been theorized that he developed a belief in reincarnation while playing the game and studying the various manuals, from which he formulated the idea or game component that if he were to kill people, he would be doing them a favor because he would be sending them to a better place. Unfortunately, there came a time when he could no longer distinguish fantasy from reality or separate the world of Dungeons and Dragons® from his everyday world. Thus the freeway became his game world (or at least a part of it).

Although cases such as these and others have not been numerous thus far, new cases are surfacing. Because of the publicity given to these cases, more people are coming forward to relate what has happened to them and their families. Parents are discovering that the experiences of their children are not rare or isolated events but similar to those of others. Former dungeon masters and players are realizing that others have had the same experiences. Researchers, gathering data from these reports, are finding that the same or similar problems have been experienced by different people. Obviously, as the number of reports increases, so also do the concerns of people.

There has also been some cause for concern over reports

that the average age of those who play has dropped considerably in recent years. In past years FRP games were popular primarily among college students and science fiction buffs; however, in a recent year, children in the 10- to 14-year-old category purchased 46 percent of all the games sold, and 15- to 17-year-olds accounted for an additional 26 percent.[4]

What sort of influence might such games have on impressionable adolescents who are still in the formative stages of their identity and personality development? Will it be, as one fan surmised, "a way of helping kids forge their identity and of preparing them to meet Huxley's Brave New World"?[5] Or could it be, as a critic commented, a way of preparing them for something perhaps even darker?

Today these concerns have intensified and reached such proportions that controversy over this game is frequently making headlines in newspapers from coast to coast. Both religious and secular observers, as well as former players, have criticized FRP games for their occultic overtones, violence, and potential for negatively affecting the lives of those who play the games.

Differences of opinion have, in some instances, caused splits in families, school boards, churches, and communities, not to mention the occasional pitting of parents against their children, pastors against their parishioners, youth pastors against their young people, young people against their peers, and even friend against friend.

Community groups such as B.A.D.D. (Bothered About Dungeons & Dragons) and others have been formed to combat this game and warn people of its dangers. National groups such as Pro Family Forum and others have also taken a strong stand against it.

There is no doubting that FRP games such as Dungeons and Dragons® are enmeshed in a sea of controversy. To un-

4. Geoffrey Smith, "Dungeons and Dollars," *Forbes*, 15 September 1980, p. 139.
5. Johnston, p. 34.

derstand something of this situation that has developed as a result of the concerns of many, one need only survey a cross section of our population or peruse a variety of articles, both pro and con, that have been published in newspapers and magazines. The broad spectrum of comments and diversity of opinions will probably be similar to at least some of the following:

"Dungeons and what?"

"It's a game."

"It's an excursion into the world of fantasy and imagination."

"It's no worse than chess, and better than Monopoly.®"

"D & D is nothing but Tolkien visualized and certainly is no more harmful than a Tolkien fantasy—and is more interesting and captivating besides."

"Dungeons and Dragons® is an educational tool that has helped our son to be more creative and assertive."

"It's an addictive game that provides escape from the everyday world of reality through fantasy."

"D & D teaches sorcery and voodoo and is a demonic, occult, pagan, witch-loving game of the devil."

"The most effective, most magnificently packaged, most profitable marketed, most thoroughly researched introduction to the occult in recorded history."

"That game caused great depression and despair in our son's life and almost brought him to the point of suicide."

"It was the cause of our son's death."

"Who cares!"

It seems from the above that we would, in general, be correct in saying there are two major camps in existence today when it comes to the subject of fantasy role-playing games: those who think they are harmless (or helpful) and those who do not. Some in the first camp, having heard the concerns of others, have simply rationalized away those concerns as the paranoia of uninformed or unimaginative people. Few have attempted to grapple with specific cases involving FRP-related problems. When they do, they have usually sought to explain away any FRP involvement as circumstantial. Some might admit to Dungeons and Dragons® as a "contributing" factor in a particular case, but it appears to be out of the question that a game could be the "cause." Obviously, responses thus far from the first camp have not been acceptable to those in the second. For them, this evidence still stands. And so the controversy continues.

What about fantasy role-playing games? Are they *just* games, as some believe? Or are they more?

Dungeons and Dragons®:
Its Origin and Adventure

2

Dungeons and Dragons®: Its Origin and Adventure

Begin with some war games in which players plan strategies and re-create battles, with the option of altering their outcomes. Specialize in the campaigns and crusades of the medieval period. Then include some elements from mythology and some action from the great "swords and sorcery" classics and stir briskly until they begin to form a medieval world of myth and fantasy. Now add a maze of tunnels, caves, chambers, and antechambers (perhaps even some different time periods, worlds, and dimensions), a good number of weapons and spells, a lot of monsters, fiends, orcs, goblins, dragons, demons, ghosts, and spirits, a few traps, and some treasure. Mix it all together, and you have the basic recipe for one of the most popular games in America today—Dungeons and Dragons®. Of course the uniqueness of each playing session or campaign is largely dependent on the quality and quantity of the various ingredients selected by the dungeon master.

How Did It All Begin?

D & D had its beginning as a spinoff of war games. Back in the late 1950s and '60s, games like Gettysburg and Bismarck, which involve the use of strategy and the playing out of historical battles with miniature soldiers, were the interest of the day. Many were attracted to these games and the idea behind them, and as a result war-gaming became somewhat fashionable.

As interest grew, an International Federation of Wargaming was formed to provide some overall organization. Under its umbrella were a number of special interest groups or societies including the "Castle and Crusade Society" (C & C Society). Gary Gygax was not only the founder of this society but the publisher of its magazine *Domesday Book* as well.

In one of the early issues, Gygax "drew a map of the 'Great Kingdom' " so that "members of the society could then establish their holdings on the map."[1] Dave Arneson was one of the first to claim an area. He established a barony, Blackmoor, in the northeast section just above the Great Kingdom and began his campaign there with other players in the Twin Cities (Minneapolis-St. Paul). Other members soon followed suit.

During this time, when campaigns were being waged in different areas, Gygax claims he and Robert Kuntz came up with the idea that it might be fun "to play some games which would reflect the action of the great swords and sorcery yarns." "So," he says, "I devised such rules, and the Lake Geneva (Wisconsin) Tactical Studies Association proceeded to play-test them."[2]

Arneson began to incorporate these rules into his campaign and, within a relatively short period of time, developed a modified fantasy version in which, according to Gygax,

1. Gary Gygax, "Gary Gygax on Dungeons & Dragons," in *Best of the Dragon* (Lake Geneva, Wis.: TSR Periodicals, 1980), p. 29.
2. Ibid.

players began as Heroes or Wizards. With sufficient success they could become Superheroes. In a similar fashion, Wizards could become more powerful. Additionally, he had added equipment for players to purchase and expanded the character descriptions considerably—even adding several new masters.[3]

Commenting on Arneson's modifications, Gygax says, "The idea of a measured progression (experience points) and the addition of games taking place in a dungeon maze struck me as being very desirable."[4]

A few weeks later Gygax, working from the rules and notes he had received from Arneson, developed the "Greyhawk" campaign (the very first Dungeons and Dragons® campaign). "Greyhawk" was play-tested at the Lake Geneva Tactical Studies Association. Manuscript copies of the campaign were sent to players in various areas for their comments. At this point, explains Gygax, "Dungeons and Dragons had been born."[5]

Gygax admits that "although D & D was not Dave's (Arneson's) game system by any form or measure, he was given co-billing as author for his valuable idea kernels. He complained bitterly that the game was not right, but the other readers and players loved it."[6]

The "Greyhawk" campaign was published by TSR Games, Inc. (now TSR Hobbies, Inc.), of Lake Geneva, Wisconsin. TSR is the publisher and manufacturer of all Dungeons and Dragons® materials and is the largest corporation in the adventure gaming industry. TSR is continually working on the refinement of the game. Gygax says, "You can, however, rest assured that work on a complete revision of the game is in progress, and I promise a far better product."[7] At the same time TSR is busily involved in developing new modules and playing aids.

3. Ibid.
4. Ibid.
5. Ibid.
6. Ibid.
7. Ibid.

With an ever-increasing amount of paraphernalia, many bearing the inscription "Official Playing Aid Approved for D & D," playing the game can get expensive. The basic package—the dice and introductory booklet—costs $10 and does not take the player very far. True indulgence in the game requires the purchasing and mastering of such books as the *Player's Handbook, Dungeon Master's Guide, The Monster Manual,* and *Deities and Demigods.* In addition to these books, many other accessories are available for purchase: scenarios, grid sheets, intricately detailed and painted miniatures, special ivories (dice), and so on. There are presently over one hundred different booklets and accessories that can be bought for a total cost in excess of $500.

How Is It Played?

Dungeons and Dragons® is an elaborate fantasy game played essentially in the mind, using one's creative imagination.

In anticipation of playing, one discovers, first of all, that familiar game components such as cards and boards are not used (although there are dice). Second, there are no rules, only guidelines. One may purchase rule books or a set of rules for a campaign, but there are no rules in the game itself. The editors of one TSR publication have explained it this way: "As we've said time and time again, the 'rules' were never meant to be more than guidelines; not even true 'rules.' "[8]

Third, there is no limitation on time. Most FRP games are not single-experience contests, but ongoing campaigns or endless adventures "with each playing session related to the next by results and participant characters who go from episode to episode."[9] Thus, a single game could theoretically

---

8. Robert Kuntz and James Ward, *Gods, Demigods, and Heroes,* Supplement IV (Lake Geneva, Wis.: TSR Games, 1976), Foreword.
9. Gary Gygax, *Advanced Dungeons & Dragons Players Handbook* (Lake Geneva: Wis.: TSR Games, 1978), p. 7.

extend indefinitely. Some newspaper accounts mention games that are currently approaching five years in length. A typical playing session, however, only lasts from three to five hours. But extensions into days are not uncommon.

Fourth, there appear to be no absolutes and virtually no boundaries. This flexibility helps to extend the game further into the vast limits of human creativity and imagination, which no doubt increases its appeal and fascination. The fact that wits and imagination are crucial for success is a principal reason FRP games attract so many with above-average intelligence.[10]

Three or more players and a dungeon master are needed to play Dungeons and Dragons®. The dungeon master, or referee, is usually someone very experienced with the game. He is in control of the game and serves as the final arbiter. With the aid of maps, combat tables, monster lists, and so on, he shapes the fantasy milieu. He selects the psycho-geographical terrain the players will travel through. It may be a multilevel of dungeons, towns, other worlds, planes, and time periods. This has all been mapped out on graph paper, complete with traps, treasures, monsters, dragons, magical objects, potions, wizards, demons, and gods in the various regions.

Each player selects a character whose role he is to assume, or play. Examples of possible character choices are cleric, druid, fighter, paladin, ranger, magic user, illusionist, thief, assassin, and monk. In terms of overall usefulness, the thief is apparently one of the best characters to emulate. According to Gygax, "None of these [characters] overshadow thieves."[11]

Each character is assigned strengths and weaknesses (on a scale of 3 to 18) in six principal attributes—intelligence, dexterity, strength, creativity, charisma, and wisdom. These are determined by a toss of the dice. Since each character is

10. Ibid., p. 5.
11. Ibid., p. 7.

most adept at one particular strength, a thief desires a high dexterity rating; a fighter, strength; a magic user, intelligence; and so on, because those attributes are most useful to their professions.

Next, a racial stock is selected—dwarven, elven, gnome, half-elven, halfling, half-orc, or human. Each race has its own unique racial disposition, which becomes a part of the character.

Players must decide their characters' alignment: good, neutral, or evil. In connection with this, each player should also have a god. Gygax comments, "Serving a deity is a significant part of D & D, and all player-characters should have a patron god. Alignment assumes its full importance when tied to the working of a deity."[12]

Once the characters have been established, they have to be properly armed with weapons and equipped with supplies apropos their mission. They will each possess certain spell-casting capacities based on their class, race, and abilities.

The object of the game is for the players to maneuver their characters through the dungeon master's precarious environment, encountering and conquering various beings or entities, collecting treasures, and gathering experiences for later advancement. Verbal guidance is given by the dungeon master. The players must engage their imagination and mentally visualize each situation and every action taken in that situation as they travel through the environment. Even though each character will function in accordance with his own abilities and traits, every action is decided on collectively by the entire group of players.

It is not necessary for the game to end. It can extend indefinitely, with players repeatedly simply taking up where they left off. If a character is killed, he can be resurrected by magic or reincarnated into some other entity or character.

12. James M. Ward and Robert J. Kuntz, *Deities and Demigods: Cyclopedia of God and Heroes from Myth and Legend,* ed. Lawrence Schick (Lake Geneva, Wis.: TSR Games, 1980), p. 5.

And should all else fail, there is always the option to begin again with a new character.

There is no end to the multiple permutation of characters, dimensions, encounters, situations, and levels, which can perpetuate a fantasy environment as complicated and lengthy as imagination, dice rolls, and persistence can make it. For example, a sixth-rank thief could encounter a fourth-order demon on the tenth dungeon level and render it helpless with a fifth-power magical spell as he winds his way through successively complex dimensions stretching toward infinity. Or, a gnome could invoke a nnuuurrr'c'c (a deadly 40-foot tall mosquito with a 140-foot wingspan) from the astral plane to attack and kill a half-orc as it makes its lengthy journey to "middle earth."

Two Basic Questions

Role playing certainly has come a long way in the past decade or so. Its evolution from war games based on history to swords-and-sorcery games set within a world of mythology, fantasy, and magic not only has revolutionized the adventure gaming industry, it also has provoked the raising of at least two very basic but crucial concerns.

First of all, these games are, by nature, role-playing games. In the past, players assumed the roles of soldiers or other related characters. Today they assume the roles of what some have referred to as more "unsavory" characters—for example, a thief, assassin, or magic user. Furthermore, in the past, although imagination was necessary, the tendency was toward mere role playing. Today, intense imagination is required, and the tendency now appears to be in the direction of developing an alter ego, which grows and develops as the player's imagination is being experienced.

What effect will all this have on the player's life and in the development of his self-image and personality? Some proponents of the game have responded by saying, "Nothing more than the effect on children playing cops and robbers." But the possibility of carrying one's role playing into everyday life is always present, even in cops and robbers. If one learns to be a robber as a result of playing the role of a robber, or develops some negative traits (e.g., shoplifting or stealing change from his parents), would that not be cause for concern? The chances of becoming a thief, an assassin, an occultist (magic user), or of developing some negative traits and characteristics may be far greater in FRP games simply because of the prolongation and development of the game's character as the player's alter ego.

Second, these games are, by nature, set within a world view. In the past, role-playing games had a historical setting. Today it is one of fantasy and mythology. Furthermore, there is no denying that in the past violence and the quest for power were part of the games; but today there is that and much more (immorality, idolatry, and occultism). What effect might all this have in the development of a player's personal philosophy and morality?

Unfortunately, most players participate without ever considering the world view in which they are role playing. Nor do they consider how contrary it may be to their own philosophy and beliefs. Because of their involvement, players generally will not even notice any changes that may be occurring in their own lives as a result of playing the game (although their parents or peers may notice some changes).

Perhaps at this point it would be good to stand back from the game and to consider the world view of FRP games before beginning our evaluation.

The Theology of
Fantasy Role-Playing Games

3

The Theology of Fantasy Role-Playing Games

When one begins to explore the various fantasy role-playing (FRP) games that are available today, one quickly discovers that each game has its own distinctiveness—that is, some game paraphernalia, characters, elements, settings, and so forth, that are different from those in other games. More important, however, one also discovers that each game has its own universe (world view or theology), fashioned by words and concepts that work together to provide a more or less coherent frame of reference for all thought and action. It is within this framework that all meaning and understanding regarding the game is derived. Therefore, players must comprehend the game's universe in order to understand fully their role playing and be able to assess that in which they are involved.

Although there is some diversity among FRP games, and therefore among FRP universes, there appear also to be a number of common elements. Our interest in this chapter lies particularly with those elements that will provide a basis for the discussion presented in the preceding and succeeding chapters. Those elements are set forth below and compared and contrasted with the biblical teaching on the subject. By doing this, it is hoped that similarities and differences can be more easily noted by the Christian and that any non-Christian reader will have a clearer understanding of where Christians (including the authors) stand in their perception and assessment of these games.

GOD

FRP games in general posit a theology known as polytheism—the belief in many gods. "No fantasy world would be complete," says one game manual, "without the gods, mighty deities who influence the fate of men and move mortals about like chesspieces in their obscure games of powers."[1]

In these games, each player is expected to have a patron god and to have some contact with his deity.[2] Furthermore, one is often required to "appease" his deity and, on occasion, may even have to provide some "atonement" (e.g., "several days of fasting, prayer, and meditation and/or minor sacrifices"[3]).

The Bible posits a theology known as monotheism—the belief in only one God (Deuteronomy 6:4; Isaiah 43:10; 44:6, 8; 1 Corinthians 8:4). According to the Bible, God is One, yet eternally exists in three Persons: the Father, the Son, and the Holy Spirit.

Scriptures say there are many things that are called gods, but there is by nature only one true God—the God of the Bible (1 Corinthians 8:5-6; Galatians 4:8). Therefore, the Bible expressly forbids the pursuit of any other god or gods

1. James M. Ward and Robert J. Kuntz, *Deities and Demigods: Cyclopedia of Gods and Heroes from Myth and Legend,* ed. Lawrence Schick (Lake Geneva, Wis.: TSR Games, 1980), p. 37.
2. Gary Gygax, *Advanced Dungeons and Dragons Players Handbook* (Lake Geneva, Wis.: TSR Games, 1978), pp. 49, 80.
3. Ward, pp. 9-10.

(Exodus 20:3-5). God loves us and desires that we have a personal relationship with Him.

CREATION

FRP games generally put forth a nontheistic universe or universes—that is, without an infinite creator God. On rare occasions a few games appear to allude to some substance or substances (such as air, earth, fire, and water) as the basic "stuff" everything is made of, but almost all the games seem to set forth a number of parallel universes and planes of existence without any concern or reference to their composition or origin.[4]

The Bible posits a theistic universe or universes, one that begins with the personal, infinite God who created "the heavens and the earth" out of nothing (Genesis 1:1). What He created is distinct from His essence and being, and yet He works within the created space-time continuum.

MAN

Most FRP games say that man can better himself and progress through various levels by means of cooperation, skill, and some luck. In these games a player can begin as a hero or wizard and in time become a superhero, and so on. Should he become insolent toward his deity or make mistakes during his journey through life, he can always make "atonement" for those.

In some games it is even possible to attain to the level of divinity or deity (but this usually takes years—many years—to accomplish). "As study of the various mythologies will show," says one such game manual, "it is remotely possible for mortals to ascend into the rank of the divine."[5] That man-

4. For example, Gygax, pp. 120-21.
5. Ward, p. 74.

ual goes on to discuss the various requirements necessary for attaining the divine level, and also a consequence—". . . ascension to divinity effectively removes the character from the general campaign."[6]

The Bible states that man has disobeyed God, thus alienating himself from God (Romans 3:23). Payment for sin, or atonement, is needed, but sinful man is incapable of providing this. God loves man so much that He took the initiative in history by sending His Son, Jesus Christ, the second Person of the Godhead, to die for our sins (John 3:16; 1 John 4:10). His death on the cross paid the penalty for mankind's sins (Romans 5:8-11; Hebrews 9:26; 10:12, 18). Jesus rose bodily from the dead and lives today.

According to the Bible, Jesus Christ alone is the only way to life and to God (John 14:6; Acts 4:12). Jesus said, "He who believes in the Son has eternal life; but he who does not obey the Son shall not see life, but the wrath of God abides on him" (John 3:36). A person must recognize his own condition as a sinner before God, confess his sin to God, believe that Jesus died on the cross as payment for his sins (Jesus Himself being without sin), and trust in Jesus Christ as Lord and Savior to be reconciled to God and forgiven.

RESURRECTION/REINCARNATION

FRP games in general posit at least two options for man regarding immortality. One option is resurrection. In these games, this is merely the revival of a person after death by use of such magical means as "spells of resurrection"[7] or a "rod of resurrection." Another option is reincarnation. This is the bringing back of a person after death in a new incarnation (in another body) by use of such magical means as "reincarnation spells."[8]

6. Ibid.
7. Gygax, pp. 50, 53.
8. Ibid., pp. 64, 68.

The Bible tells of only one conclusion for man—resurrection. (Resurrection and reincarnation are incompatible with each other.) God made man as a psychosomatic unity (a physical and spiritual being). Man has not only a soul (and/or spirit) but a body that is destined for resurrection one day. Our resurrection is guaranteed by the resurrection of Jesus Christ from the dead, and it will occur at the time of His return to this earth (Romans 8:23-24; 1 Corinthians 15; 1 John 3:2-3).

MORALITY

FRP games generally see an amoral universe at best. Good and evil seem to be presented as equal and opposite poles. In these games, both the characters and the gods are required or expected to align themselves with one pole or the other. Good and evil can be complementary or in conflict with each other. Because these games are open-ended, there is no final victory for good or evil.[9]

Such activitites as rape, stealing, murder, mutilation, human sacrifices, and so forth are incorporated into the adventure of the games. The situation itself and the characters involved determine what should or should not be done (as well as what is right or wrong).

The Bible posits a moral universe. God not only is the source of the physical world (as we have already noted) but the moral world as well.

Morality is grounded in God's goodness. Thus there is an absolute standard by which all moral judgments can be measured. God has revealed this standard to us in the various

9. TSR Hobbies, Inc., the manufacturer of Dungeons and Dragons® (D & D), has an in-house document entitled "TSR Code of Ethics" in which explicit instructions are given us to know "good should always triumph over evil." However, neither this document nor this conclusion has been made public in or with any of the games or manuals manufactured by TSR. (This was discussed on "The 700 Club" TV program, June 13, 1984.)

laws and principles expressed in His Word, the Bible. These laws and principles are given for our instruction that we might know what is right and what ought to be done in a given situation.

Conclusion

It is obvious from the above discussion that the theology found in FRP games is quite different from biblical theology. From the initial differences regarding the Creator and the creation right down to the end-time product, they are definitely two distinct and contrary theologies. It should also be obvious to all that the theology found in these games is an outright denial of much (if not all) of biblical theology.

Do FRP games have a theology one should believe in and commit his life to? Are the doctrines and practices those that one should participate in—even in role playing? If one should start to become his game character in reality, or if one should bring aspects from the theology (whether doctrines or practices) into everyday life, would the effects be positive or negative?

Finally, if the theology found in these games is not true and there is a false understanding of the supernatural, then the gods and demons one calls upon and imagines may not at times be purely imaginative and nonexistent after all. And if, as the Bible indicates, there are real spirit beings called demons, would that make any difference?

Black, White, or a Mixture of Grays?

4

Black, White, or a Mixture of Grays?

$\mathbf{A}$ high school student one day asked her teacher what she thought of fantasy role-playing (FRP) games. With a smile, the teacher said she would enjoy playing because it would allow her to use her imagination. She was also told that her creative and analytical abilities, as well as her mathematical skills, would be enhanced by playing this game. Another teacher, overhearing the conversation, could not in good conscience allow this student to play what he perceived to be an evil game. He decided to interrupt and give his opinion (which was really a tirade) about the game's occultic content. The student could do nothing but stand there and watch two teachers she respected argue, but in the end she was left with her original question.

Are all FRP games, including Dungeons and Dragons®, good? Some, like the first teacher, are convinced they are harmless excursions into fantasy on the same level as a Tolkien novel. Others are equally convinced that such games are evil and demonic. Or are FRP games perhaps a mixture of grays?

Answering the student's question is not as easy as one might expect, regardless of one's initial persuasion. In the real world there are usually two or more sides to an issue, and FRP games are no exception. To categorically declare that all FRP games are "evil" and "of the devil" would be simplistic and erroneous. But to accept all of them uncritically as "good" or "harmless" would also be simplistic and erroneous—and could lead to some undesirable consequences. How can a person make an intelligent assessment of these games?

In critically examining FRP games, at least four basic areas should be considered: (1) the role of fantasy, (2) morality, (3) escapism, and (4) occultism. Collectively, these should determine the conclusion about any FRP game. In the first and third areas (fantasy and escapism), there is possibility for either good or evil, for benefit or harm. This is largely determined by content, duration, and motive. In the second and fourth areas (morality and occultism), there is less room for possibilities. In those two areas, from a Christian perspective, anything that denies biblical morality or supports occultism could not be considered spiritually healthy. In fact, it is potentially harmful to the individual as well as to society.

In this chapter we will look at the first three areas: fantasy, morality, and escapism. The fourth area, occultism, will be discussed in chapter 5.

Fantasy

It should be understood from the outset that there is nothing wrong with fantasy per se.

Fantasy, in its essence, is an imaginative departure from the world and the created order of things as we know it. It plays an important part in our lives. Who can doubt that a child's imagination in play, even in role playing, is a positive component of his social and intellectual development? It also exerts an important psychological role in the life of an adolescent or adult, whether it be daydreaming about a fishing trip or vacation, stretching the boundaries of one's imagination and talented creativity in the arts and literature, or some escapist relaxation. Everyone has experienced enjoyment in and positive use of his imagination and fantasies at one time or another.

Fantasy is actually a part of God's creation in the sense that God created man with imagination and the ability to fantasize. Support for this can be derived from the biblical doctrine of the image of God. As Elliot Miller explains:

> A defense can be made in favor of such an exercise of the imagination on the grounds that man is created in the image of God, and thus, like God, is creative. Because man is not God, he cannot create things out of nothing. However because he is like God, he can create objects in the real world (such as a home, an automobile, or a computer) by utilizing raw material out of God's creation. Another aspect of man's creativity is his ability, by his imagination, to create secondary worlds where things are different than in the primary world. Though he does not have the power to bring these worlds into actual substance, if he succeeds at achieving what J. R. R. Tolkien has termed "an inner consistency of reality," others may, through their imaginations, attain a state of "secondary belief," where they are able to perceive and appreciate the invented reality.[1]

But fantasy is not justified in itself. Just because fantasy in general is part of God's creation, no specific fantasy is necessarily right or good. As with many other things in God's creation, there are good and bad uses. Unfortunately, even "good" fantasy can be corrupted by overindulgence (e.g., when a person enters a fantasy world to escape from responsibilities in the everyday world). There is also a distorted and destructive use (e.g., the fantasizing of sexual exploits or extreme violence toward someone).

1. Brian Onken and Elliot Miller, "Dungeons and Dragons," *Forward* 4, no. 2:13.

Determining a good use of fantasy from a bad use is at the heart of the controversy today with FRP games. Proponents of Dungeons and Dragons®, in their attempt to establish that this game constitutes a legitimate use of fantasy, have created parallels between it and certain Christian fantasy writings. Then they say (either explicitly or by implication), "If one accepts the fantasy works of J. R. R. Tolkien, C. S. Lewis, and others as a good and right use of fantasy, one should also accept D & D." Consider, for example the following excerpt from a letter to the editor of *Christianity Today* in which an Episcopalian minister defends his endorsement of Dungeons and Dragons®:

> It may be too much to suggest that any given game is the "creative enactment of a Tolkien fantasy." But by the same token, D & D derives its force and attraction by the same dynamic typical of great literature. In D & D we are literally drawn into the battle between good and evil, order and chaos. If the characters and situations become enthralling, how does this differ from reading a Tolkien story, or one of the Chronicles of Narnia, or L'Engles' "A Wrinkle in Time"?[2]

On the surface, this argument appears to have some credibility, for there is at least something of a parallel between certain fantasy games and certain Christian fiction (e.g., Tolkien). That such works as Tolkien's *Lord of the Rings,* Lewis's space trilogy, and the novels of Charles Williams require the existence of good and evil, intense adventures, the experience of fantasy environments and worlds, and mythological beings cannot be denied. Several of those works have elements different from (and thus, inevitably, sometimes contrary to) the world as God made it. Some have incorporated magic and sorcery into their fantasy and, on occasion, portrayed the magic and spells in a fashion contrary to the Bible.

2. *Christianity Today,* 2 October 1981, p. 10.

But although there are some common elements, there are also some great differences, which proponents of FRP games either ignore or rationalize away. Christian fantasy works by Tolkien, Lewis, and others are accepted and considered to be a good use of fantasy because they offer a reflection of an essentially Christian world view. As one researcher explains:

> In wholesome fantasy we will find that its creator will have infused into his "universe" an inherent morality, which parallels that of the actual universe, as explained in the Bible.
>
> Though in a fantasy world there may be such a thing as "good magic," though there may be talking beasts and mythic creatures, in back of it all there must still be (whether revealed explicitly or alluded to implicitly) a supreme being who provides a basis for authentic morality. Absolute morality can only be sustained in a theistic universe; a universe governed by a transcendent holy God. In such a world good and evil are consistent and final for all creatures of conscience, rather than fluctuating according to the differing mores of the creatures themselves. As Tolkien's hero Aragorn affirms in *The Two Towers* (p. 50), "Good and ill have not changed since yesteryear; nor are they one thing among Elves and Dwarves and another among Men."[3]

Though the creators of Dungeons and Dragons® may have borrowed many aspects from Tolkien's "middle earth," one part they did not consider was the overall setting in which everything took place and from which everything derived its ultimate meaning—Tolkien's Christian world view. As a result, the game's world view does not represent the moral universe God created. In place of the creator God, its universe is governed by a multiplicity of gods and demigods. Moreover, its universe is not infused with an absolute, inherent morality.

The more thoroughly one investigates the writings of Tol-

3. Onken and Miller, p. 13.

kien, Lewis, and others and compares them to FRP games, the more one will see that there are not only crucial differences in the theological and moral perspectives but also in the context and motives of their respective inventors. Furthermore, there are important differences in the kind and extent of participation required in each (e.g., the cultivation of fantasy in the participatory amoral milieu of Dungeons and Dragons® versus the passive moral universe of Tolkien).

In conclusion, *neither fantasy nor fantasy role playing is wrong in and of itself.* When carried out within the context of the Christian world view, it can serve as a useful and creative activity. We are creatures made in the image of an imaginative God, and we should consider it a privilege to possess and exercise this precious gift of imaginaton. But we must also realize our obligation before God to use this gift in a wholesome way and to guard against any misuse.

Discerning the difference between a wholesome use and misuse begins with the question "To what end or for what purpose [is the imagination] being exercised in a particular direction?"[4] This certainly appears to be the question Jesus had in mind in His Sermon on the Mount when He stated, "Every one who looks on a woman to lust for her has committed adultery with her already in his heart" (Matthew 5:28). If Jesus taught that lust is tantamount to adultery (which God condemns—see Deuteronomy 5:18; 22:13-27), would He approve of the deliberate cultivation and enjoyment of fantasy regarding other things that God condemns? Obviously not. To fantasize about those things that God has forbidden in His Word (immorality, the occult, the pursuit of other deities—all elements of Dungeons and Dragons®) is tantamount to doing them. This cannot be understood in any other way than a misuse of our God-given imagination. With the Bible as our guide, this is what we as Christians must guard against "so

---

4. Stanley Dokupil, *Dungeons and Dragons* (Berkeley, Calif.: Spiritual Counterfeits Project, 1982), p. 3.

that (we) may walk in a manner worthy of the Lord, to please Him in all respects" (Colossians 1:10).

MORALITY

Whether or not one likes to admit it, moral considerations play a central role in the universes created by fantasy role-playing games.

In these games, good and evil are generally presented as equal and opposite impersonal poles, with the gods as well as the characters (players) aligning themselves with one or the other. There are no moral absolutes, nor are there any moral conclusions. Good does not triumph over evil in the end, and even in the interim, good is no better than evil—it is just one tool in the conquest. Good and evil are simply the instruments for survival and personal glory. Thus the end is not a moral universe but merely an amoral victory for uncertain ends. Since power and pragmatism are necessary for winning, the end justifies the means. In such a universe brute strength and cunning are exalted within the moral context that animates and allows them victory.

It is true that each player brings to the game his own moral standards and convictions, but it is also true that the game provides the player with the potential for laying aside his morality while playing. How very tempting and easy it is for any player to pursue the action of the game and adopt the necessary morality from the situation or moment. As one college player admits:

> In D & D, it's better to be evil. You get more advantages in being evil, and it's easier to go on and not have to think of what to do and what not to do. If for some reason, you had the idea in your head that you no longer trust someone, if you chop him down from behind—as an evil character there's no penalty for it.[5]

5. Quoted in Katherine Williams, "Dungeons and Dragons," *Cornerstone* 9, no. 52:14.

In understanding and assessing the moral aspects of these games, consideration should first be given to the element of power. These games thrive on the quest for power, and man has always craved power. FRP games apparently provide an avenue for expression and fulfillment. Consider for a moment the grandiose aspirations of the fledgling dungeon master who has just been informed by Dungeons and Dragons® creator Gary Gygax, "As the DM you are to become the Shaper of the Cosmos. It is you who will give form and content to all the universe. You will breathe life into the stillness, giving meaning and purpose to all the actions which are to follow."[6]

Is there any doubt that a dungeon master is offered powers he could never attain on earth? Referring to this power, one psychiatrist commented: "If there is a God, then a dungeon master is God."[7]

Although power is a very appealing aspect of these games, it is also one of the areas of greatest concern. It has even sparked some concern from within professional circles. One psychiatrist, seeing the power that can be seized in these games, cautioned: "If I had a child who tended toward schizophrenia, I'd never let him near D & D. There's a danger that it would reinforce feelings of grandiosity, of omnipotence. Reality and fantasy are hard enough for schizophrenics to differentiate."[8] Having said that, however, he then proceeds to soften the impact of his comments by saying, "But I doubt very much that the game causes problems."[9]

Where there is power, there is often violence, and FRP games are no exception. Even though it is claimed that at least as much opportunity exists for virtuous behavior, the level of violence in Dungeons and Dragons® and other FRP

6. Quoted in Onken and Miller, p. 10.
7. Quoted in Moira Johnston, "It's Only a Game—Or Is It?" *New West*, 25 August 1980, p. 38.
8. Ibid.
9. Ibid.

games is considerable, to say the least. Indications of this can be seen, for example, in the critical hit table from the game Arduin Grimoire:

> Dice roll: 37-38; hit location: crotch/chest; results: genitals/breast torn off, shock . . . Dice roll: 95; hit location: guts ripped out; results: 20% chance of dangling feet, die in 1—10 minutes . . . Dice roll: 100; hit location: head; results: entire head pulped and splattered over a wide area.[10]

Fortunately, not all FRP games are as gruesome or gory in detail as this game, but Dave Hargrave (Arduin Grimoire's inventor) actually defends its grisly specificity:

> It's deliberately gruesome. You have to blow a hole through that video shell the kids are encased in. They are little zombies. They don't know what pain is. They have never seen a friend taken out in a body bag in bitty pieces. They've got to understand that what they do has consequences. The world is sex. It is violence. It's going to destroy most of these kids when they leave TV-land.[11]

According to Hargrave, the purpose of his game is to prepare children for living in the real world by exposing them to the brutality of sex and violence they will probably find themselves involved in later. No one would deny that children need to be prepared for the real world, but many would disagree with his methodology, which they would describe as overly harsh and brutal.

Violence is also present in Dungeons and Dragons®. One proponent of this game, writing in *Psychology Today,* acknowledges the violence but sees nothing particularly unsettling about it.

10. Rule book, Arduin Grimoire, vol. 1:60.
11. Quoted in Johnston, p. 39.

> The level of violence in this make believe world runs high. There is hardly a game in which the players do not indulge in murder, arson, torture, rape, or highway robbery. . . . I don't think this imaginary violence is any more likely to warp the minds of the participants than is the endless stream of violence in TV, movies, or literature. Quite possibly, it provides for a healthy outlet for those people who are imaginative and inclined to enjoy the game.[12]

Of course, his conclusion as to the effect of "imaginary violence" would not be accepted by everyone. There are many today who are concerned about such violence, whether on television or in fantasy games specializing in emotional participation.

Where there is power and violence, there is often sexual immorality, and that certainly is true for many FRP games. The toss of the dice may well determine in some cases whether or not a character remains a virgin; and rape is not an uncommon occurrence in these games. In Dungeons and Dragons®, for example, "non-human soldiers" are expected to "rape freely at every chance."[13]

Much of the moral makeup of FRP games is dependent upon the nature of the particular game and the moral world view of the inventor. The moral nature of the game is conditioned by the fact that in acting out personal roles, moral or immoral decisions (whether by chance or not) must constantly be made for the game to continue. In this sense, *the participant creates his own moral or immoral universe.* It is this personal creation of a "moral" universe within an amoral context that is of greatest concern, because the creation or acceptance of moral choices in fantasy and in the real world may both be part of what is essentially a unitary process in personal moral development.

12. John E. Holmes, "Confessions of a Dungeon Master," *Psychology Today,* November 1980, p. 88.
13. Gary Gygax, *Dungeons and Dragons Players Handbook* (Lake Geneva, Wis.: TSR Games, 1975), p. 31.

One might raise a question here about reading fantasy literature or watching a movie or a television program. Are not the readers and viewers participating? How is that different from participation in FRP games? When one reads fantasy writings, though he is engaged in reading, his involvement is relatively passive. A moral system thrown at him from the book is filtered through his moral standards. But in FRP games, the involvement is participatory. He is not merely identifying with a character, or hero, as in a book—he is the hero.

Movies and television are more visually participatory than literature, but the viewer is still relatively passive. He receives input; he does not create it. As in reading literature, he filters input through his own moral standards. He may empathize dearly with a character, but he does not become that character. The essential difference between FRP games and literature, television, and the movies is that the games offer a participatory fantasy in which one does not merely read about or see a character; one actually becomes the character.

One might raise a further question at this point regarding movie and television actors. Do they not participate by acting out parts (i.e., role playing)? How is this different from that in FRP games? Actually, actors are probably more involved in their roles than any FRP game player. But they are professional role players, not impressionable adolescents caught up in the excitement of a game. They are typically men and women who have a good grip on reality to begin with. As opportunities arise, they play different roles, moving from one part to another, although some continue to play a character over a prolonged period (as in a television series). It should be admitted in all honesty, however, that since both acting and role playing have *participation* in common, some of the same potential problems in FRP games could occur when acting out a part for a movie or television program.

FRP games are, by their very nature, fantasy (imagination) and role playing (participation). The player becomes the character in a fantasy world of power, violence, and sexual immorality. He participates in that universe and must use cunning and strength to conquer. Since the player and the character are one in thought and decision, to say that something was not really the player's (thoughts of seduction, stealing, or killing) but those of the character is superbly ridiculous. There is only one person involved, and he is both the player and the character. Therefore, it has to be the player's thoughts and decisions. Now, this is not to say that a player would necessarily believe or do in real life all that he verbalizes in a game, but simply to indicate that the door is opened for wrong thoughts and decisions, as well as a loosening of his moral will.

Not only does the player become the character, but, in some of the games, the character becomes a model for all to admire and emulate. Gygax says, "The ultimate aim of the game [D & D] is to gain sufficient esteem as a good player to retire your character—he becomes a kind of mythical historical figure, someone for others to look up to and admire."[14] Are thieves, rapists, assassins, and magic users (occultists) of the moral sort that others, especially children, should be encouraged to admire, to accept as "models"? Should everyone follow their example and use cunning and power, right or wrong—including violence and sexual immorality—to become an important figure? What kind of morality is being modeled here for us, and where is the dividing line between that which is moral and that which is not?

From a moral perspective, both the participatory element of the game and the exemplary aspect of the characters leave much to be desired. The process of formulating moral decisions in FRP has the potential to affect the process in the real world, simply because of the unity of the player and character. But it also has the exemplary attraction to affect moral decisions in real life because the player desires to be like his character.

14. "The Most Popular Fantasy of All," *MacLeans*, 21 April 1980.

Is there a true morality—one in which right is right and wrong is wrong, whether in fantasy or reality? The answer is yes. *There is a standard of right and wrong for everyone,* regardless of what any game may establish or person might determine for himself. That standard can be found and understood only in a moral universe created by a good and holy God, because God Himself—His character and goodness, holiness and love—is the standard.

Such a standard cannot be found in current FRP games, because their universes are essentially non-theistic. Without God as creator, there can be no basis for absolutes. Morality becomes man-centered (or, in FRP games, character-related), and right and wrong, morality and immorality, are determined by relativism and situationalism. In such universes, what is, is. Doing what is necessary or using whatever means are possible to conquer, following the alignment or abilities of one's character, being good or totally evil, are all acceptable.

Therefore, discerning the differences between right and wrong, morality and immorality, must begin with the realization that God exists and that God has revealed not only Himself but His standard in the Bible. The Ten Commandments, the Sermon on the Mount, the apostle Paul's ethical teaching—all set forth God's standards of right and wrong. In assessing FRP games, all one has to do is compare the teachings and practices in those games with the Bible. The Bible is the final authority on right and wrong, and if God declares in the Bible that prostitution, rape, stealing, mutilation, murder, human sacrifices, worshiping other gods, casting spells, using magic, and practicing necromancy are wrong, should one practice those things or become involved in a fantasy game in which one participates by imaginative role playing?

Does anyone have the authority to make right what God declares as wrong? Obviously not. Yet there are those who acknowledge God and have even accepted Jesus Christ as Lord and Savior who declare, at least by their continued participation in FRP games, that this is possible. Doing—or imagining—what God declares in His Word to be wrong cannot be understood as anything less than sin.

Inward thought life is related to outward behavior, hence the Bible's emphasis on inward purity. A sanctified thought life is the first line of defense against allowing one's thoughts to lead to sinful behavior. The unconstrained imagination may function as a catalyst or at least impetus toward sin. As Earl Wilson, a practicing psychologist and professor at Western Conservative Baptist Seminary in Portland, Oregon, states, "A behavior chain (of sin) is simply a pattern in which one thought or behavior triggers another which triggers another. In a chain of obsessional thinking, a rather innocent thought leads to one that is less innocent, which in turn leads to more dangerous thoughts and behavior until acting on the obsession is complete."[15]

Can anyone believe then that the imagining of sinful behavior, as in certain FRP games, is simply an innocent pastime?

With the Bible as our guide, we must first of all guard our minds against wrong thoughts. Images, concepts, and ideas that are introduced to the consciousness will have consequences in actions. And, second, we must guard ourselves against wrong decisions and actions. The apostle Paul summarized this beautifully when he wrote:

> Whatever is true, whatever is honorable, whatever is right, whatever is pure, whatever is lovely; whatever is of good repute, if there is any excellence and if anything worthy of praise, let your mind dwell on these things.
>
> The things you have learned and received and heard and seen in me, practice these things; and the God of peace shall be with you. (Philippians 4:8-9)

15. Earl Wilson, "Counseling the Sexually Obsessed," *Leadership*, Spring 1984, p. 48.

Escapism

Escape is best understood in our context as the freeing of one's self from the custody and restraints of the real world. Since the predominant way of escape from reality is through fantasy and the imagination, one can assume there is at least some correlation between fantasy and escape.

As with fantasy, there is nothing intrinsically wrong with escape. It is a necessary component of life. When used properly, it can be refreshing and wholesome. When misused, it can make a negative impact on one's life.

Proponents of fantasy role-playing games argue that escape is exactly what these games provide. As one dungeon master said:

> For a few hours, everyone agrees to accept the world, to accept your pretense that you are a magician who can throw exploding balls of fire from your hand. The fantasy has become a reality, a sort of giant *folie a deux* or shared reality.[16]

Proponents say that FRP games provide a wholesome form of escape, one that can be beneficial to the player.

No one would deny that FRP games provide an adventuresome form of escape from reality. But one of the complaints most frequently voiced by critics is that players have taken advantage of this form of escape and have abused it.

What aspects of escape can be misused or abused? First of all, there is time. According to Gary Gygax, "The most extensive requirement (in Dungeons and Dragons®) is time."[17] There is only so much time in each day, week, month, year—in a lifetime. As stewards of time, each should make the best use of the time he has. For many (if not most) players, FRP games typically steal valuable time from other activities that

16. Holmes, p. 93.
17. Gary Gygax, *Dungeons and Dragons* basic manual (Lake Geneva: Wis.: TSR Hobbies, 1979), p. 3.

are far more important to the lives of the players than any alleged benefits from the games. It is not uncommon to hear reports of games that have continued throughout the night or for days at a time. And it appears that, for at least some players, the more time one spends playing the game, the more time the game demands. One player in his fourth year of play expressed it this way: "I tried to stop but it refused to stop."[18] In escape, then, one area of potential abuse is time—time taken from other activities.

Second, there is a potential misuse of identification. When escaping via FRP games, one usually becomes a character in a fantasy. The goal of such participation is to play the role of that character to perfection. But while doing that, the player is also expected to remember that, in reality, he is not the character. Only in fantasy is he the character.

The problem comes when a player takes his fantasy role too seriously. One player, describing this phenomenon, ex-plains:

> When a character dies, a piece of you goes away. . . . I've seen people literally go into fits because a character was killed or injured. As if they themselves had actually been hurt. They scream, shout, plead, beg, anything, just don't kill my charac-ter, don't let him die.[19]

One mother said, "I've seen people have fits, yell for fifteen minutes, hurl dice at a grand piano when their character dies."[20] In escape fantasy, another potential danger is over-identification with the character—the player actually be-comes the character.

Third, there is a potential misuse of reality. When escaping into the fantasy world of FRP games, that fantasy world can be far more exciting and usually much better than the every-

18. Quoted in Onken and Miller, p. 9.
19. Quoted in Williams p. 14.
20. Quoted in Johnston, p. 39.

day world of reality. The desire to become part of that fantasy has led some to make the imaginary world their "reality." As a result, the real world becomes less and less real. The following commentary on life by a young man appears to illustrate all of this beautifully, but tragically.

> I am dungeon master 98 percent of the time. I am the God of my world, the creator who manipulates the gods and humans. . . . When I'm in my world, I control my own world order. I can picture it all. The groves and trees. The beauty. I can hear the wind. The world isn't like that . . . school seems increasingly boring and droll. Your grades drop. The more time you spend in your fantasy world, the more you want to walk away from the burdensome decisions in life. . . . The more I play D & D, the more I want to get away from this world. The whole thing is getting very bad.[21]

Once the line of demarcation between fantasy (the game world) and reality is blurred, fantasy becomes more real, and the player's everyday life is affected. One former FRP fan who had traveled to Michigan in an attempt to help find Egbert, later returned home condemning FRP: "When a kid gets addicted to FRP, you see a lethargy occur in real life. Reality is sacrificed for imagination. His room, his house aren't so clean."[22]

There may be other areas of misuse and abuse in escape fantasy, but time, identification, and reality are the ones most frequently mentioned.

In conclusion, *there is nothing evil or wrong with escape per se.* Escape connected with fantasy is part of God's creation. When used correctly, it can provide a refreshing break from the pressures, stress, and anxiety of the everyday world. It is necessary for our health and well-being. But when misused or abused, it is no longer healthy.

---

21. Ibid., p. 38.
22. Ibid.

Discerning a correct use of escape begins with an assessment of our time. How much time is spent in FRP? Is that time taken from other important activities that could or should have been done? It also includes an assessment of our understanding of the difference between fantasy and reality. How real does the game or the character become to you? What effect is the fantasy world having on your everyday world? In guarding against the misuse of time and reality, we need to "be careful how (we) walk, not as unwise men, but as wise, making the most of (our) time, because the days are evil" (Ephesians 5:15-16).

The Occult Connection

5

The Occult Connection

The occult is without doubt the area of greatest concern in any discussion of such fantasy role-playing (FRP) games as Dungeons and Dragons®. Some who are knowledgeable in occult matters have indicated that near genuine, if not genuine, occult powers, spells, and practices can be found in much of the FRP literature. One occultist, Philip Emmens Isaac Bonewitz, considered Dungeons and Dragons® such a good introduction to the occult that he wrote a book to show players how they could move on into real sorcery.[1]

Let us now examine the occultic content of FRP games. The following is but a smattering of what may be found.

EXAMPLES OF OCCULTISM IN FRP GAMES

First, occult *magic and the casting of spells* can be found as an integral part of most games. In Dungeons and Dragons®,

---

1. Philip Emmens Isaac Bonewitz, *Authentic Thaumaturgy: A Professional Occultist on Improving the Realism of Magic Systems in Fantasy Stimulating Games* (Berkeley, Calif.: Chaosium, Inc., 1980). This book is no longer in print.

magic is prevalent and can be used in a variety of ways. For example, witch magic can be used for white or black witch-craft[2] (a delineation that is true in witchcraft today). There is also a preponderance of spells for different characters, levels, categories, and expectations. Some spells are bestowed by the gods; others are not. Most spells have a verbal component, which means they must be spoken to be effective.[3] Much of what is presented is similar to what one would find in sorcery or witchcraft.

In Chivalry & Sorcery, the game manual contains instructions on how to cast spells.

Second, occult forms of *protective inscriptions* can be found in certain games. The "magic circle, pentagram, and thaumaturgic triangle" have all been incorporated into Dungeons and Dragons®.[4] Players are taught how to use these symbols as forms of protective inscriptions in a fashion similar to the way they are actually used in witchcraft and Satanism. In one account, for example, a spell caster, who has just summoned a demon, is warned that he "must be within a circle of protection (or a thaumaturgic triangle with protection from evil) and the demon confined with a pentagram (circle pentacle) if he or she is to avoid being slain or carried off by the summoned cacodemon."[5]

Third, the occult practice of *astral projection, or soul travel,* can be found in a few games. In astral projection, as in certain occultic, Eastern, and eclectic groups, it is believed that a soul can depart from the body and travel to other dimensions and planes. According to Dungeons and Dragons®, this practice is possible by various means, including specific magic spells and psionic disciplines. Thus, a cleric can, by

2. Gary Gygax, "The Dungeons & Dragons Magic System," *The Best of the Dragon* (Lake Geneva, Wis.: TSR Periodicals, 1980), pp. 58-59.
3. Gary Gygax, *Advanced Dungeons and Dragons Players Handbook* (Lake Geneva, Wis.: TSR Games, 1978), p. 40.
4. Gary Gygax, *Dungeons and Dragons Players Handbook* (Lake Geneva, Wis.: TSR Games, 1975), p. 112.
5. Gygax, *Advanced Dungeons and Dragons Players Handbook,* pp. 86-87.

casting a seventh level *astral spell* project his or her astral body into the *Astral Plane,* leaving his or her physical body and material possession behind on the Prime Material Plane, (the plane on which the entire universe and all of its parallels have existence) . . . The cleric then leaves the Astral Plane, forming a body on the plane of existence he or she has chosen to enter.[6]

Fourth, the occult practice of *necromancy, communication with the dead,* can be found in many games. In Dungeons and Dragons®, necromantic spells not only heal wounds, restore strength, limbs, and life, and resurrect the dead, but they also bring forth the dead for divinational and other purposes, in a manner similar to that in spiritism. If a cleric, for example, needs information, he knows that he may summon the dead with a spell. "Upon casting a *speak with the dead* spell the cleric is able to ask several questions of a dead creature in a set period of time and receive answers according to the knowledge of the creature."[7]

In Chivalry & Sorcery, an entire section of the game manual is devoted to necromancy. Here, as in spiritism, the necromancer is actually instructed to seek after a "spirit guide." "A Necromancer will acquire a Shadow Guide, a Spirit of the dead who was once a powerful Necromancer and acts as his Mentor. . . . To summon the Shadow Guide for advice and to be taught new spells, the Necromancer must perform a solemn ceremony. . . ."[8]

Fifth, the occult practice of *conjuration and summoning of demons and devils* can also be found in many games. The *D & D Monster Manual* has a detailed section devoted solely to demons. They are named, described (complete with an artist's sketch), and categorized according to their varying abilities and powers. Players are encouraged to use this infor-

6. Ibid., p. 52.
7. Ibid., p. 48.
8. Quoted in Ronald M. Enroth, "Fantasy Games: Is There an Occult Connection?" *Eternity,* December 1981, p. 36.

mation in conjunction with certain spells to summon these beings. Thus, a cleric, for example, using a seventh-level *gate* spell, knows that he "must name the demon, devil, demi-god, god, or similar being he or she desires to make use of the gate and come to the cleric's aid." He is also told that there is "a 100% certainty that something will step through the gate."[9]

Dungeons and Dragons® mentions demon possession as a possibility. However, if a player, for example, possesses a "mind bar," it will prevent him "from suffering telepathic influence or possession by such creatures as demons or devils.[10]

Sixth, *occult alignment with powers or deities* can be found in some of the games. This is an essential part of the games, as it has been in sorcery and witchcraft throughout the years. In Dungeons and Dragons®, the alignment of each character with good (chaotic, lawful, or neutral), neutral (chaotic, lawful, or true), or evil (chaotic, lawful, or neutral) must be determined. The character's class will help in determining this. But beyond this alignment is an alignment with some deity that the character can serve and even worship. Both dungeon masters and players are told:

> No fantasy world is complete without the gods, mighty deities who influence the fates of men and move mortals about like chesspieces in their obscure games of power. . . . They (the gods) are one of the Dungeon Master's most important tools in his or her shaping of events. The gods serve an important purpose for the players as well. Serving a deity is a significant part of AD & D (Advanced Dungeons & Dragons®), and all player characters should have a patron god. Alignment assumes its full importance when tied to the worship of a deity.[11]

9. Gygax, *Advanced Dungeons and Dragons Players Handbook,* p. 53.
10. Ibid., p. 115.
11. James M. Ward and Robert J. Kuntz, *Deities and Demigods: Cyclopedia of Gods and Heroes from Myth and Legend,* ed. Lawrence Schick (Lake Geneva, Wis.: TSR Games, 1980), p. 37.

Seventh, *the names of occult, or magic, orders* can be found in at least one game. Chivalry & Sorcery mentions such "Magical Orders" as "The Ancient Ones" (Druids), "The Kingdom of Wicca" (Classical Witchcraft), "The Company of the Dark Brotherhood," and others. Some of these names are reminiscent of real occult groups. The game manual also includes detailed instructions on how players can form their own magic, or occult, order.

In addition to the above, one can find such occult practices as abjuration (the neutralization or negation of magic, spells, and curses), clairaudience and clairvoyance (the ability to hear or see what is happening at a distance), divination (the knowledge of secret things or events by the aid of the gods), summoning of elements (earth, air, water, and fire) and arcane powers, and others. Dungeons and Dragons® even includes the primitive occult idea (and practice) of trapping the soul.[12]

However, the occult connection does not end with the manuals and materials of these games. In Dungeons and Dragons®, for example, frequent reference is made to the importance of actual investigation (i.e., library research) of the pagan, Eastern, and occult cultures from which the mythologies and deities are drawn. In fact, some games are "often accompanied by long hours of research into the cultures to be used in the dungeons."[13]

We are told in *Deities and Demigods,* "The books listed below constitute some of the references used in compiling this work. They, as well as numerous other works, contain much more detailed accounts of the gods and their divine characteristics than can be included herein. Further research is recommended to the DM [Dungeon Master] who wishes to augment the given information."[14]

Two of the books suggested are E. A. Wallis Budge's *The*

12. Gygax, *Advanced Dungeons and Dragons Players Handbook,* p. 92.
13. *San Diego Evening Tribune,* 13 October 1980.
14. Ward, *Deities and Demigods,* p. 143.

Egyptian Book of the Dead and Sir James Frazier's *The Golden Bough.* The former is a potent occultic volume chronicling ritualistic preparations and instructions for the dead in their post-mortem state; the latter, an anthropological compendium on occult practices in primitive societies.

Similarly, *Gods, Demi-Gods, and Heroes* states: "Further research and reading is recommended into all the myths presented herein. This is the merest of outlines, presented in D & D terms."[15] If "further research and reading is recommended" in the area of mythology, and mythology is defined as "dealing with the gods, demi-gods, and heroes of a particular people, usually involving the supernatural,"[16] then is this game not, in effect, encouraging its participants to concentrate their investigation on the supernatural and even occultic aspects of pagan cultures?

One might raise the question here as to how such research differs from that of a student in an anthropology course. Does he not research the same cultures? Obviously he does, but there are some important differences that should be noted. First, the scope of research is somewhat different. In Dungeons and Dragons® the primary focus of research appears to be narrow, dealing mostly with the area of the religious or supernatural, even though other aspects of culture may also be included. In an anthropology course (excluding those rare anthropology courses that specifically investigate the occultic aspects of various cultures[17]) the focus is generally much broader and involves several components, one of which is the religious.

Second, the purpose of research is quite different. In Dungeons and Dragons® the main purpose is to obtain informa-

15. Robert Kuntz and James Ward, *Gods, Demigods, and Heroes* (Lake Geneva, Wis.: TSR Games, 1976), Foreword.
16. Ibid.
17. See, for example, J. Richard Greenwell, "Academia and the Occult: An Experience at Arizona," *The Skeptical Inquirer* 5, no. 1:39-46. This article discusses the course Anthropology 298W—Witchcraft and the Occult—offered at the University of Arizona.

tion that may be useful in the researcher's fantasy role playing. As one player explained, "You try to think like your characters. . . . I'm running Inca characters now so I'm studying Inca culture."[18] In most anthropology courses the purpose is primarily for the researcher's understanding of the past and demonstration of his skills. (For some students, such research may be done purely to fulfill course requirements). Despite these differences, it should also be noted that researching occult activities in pagan societies has led at least some investigators to personal involvement in the occult.

From the handbooks and manuals associated with fantasy role-playing games to the recommended collateral reading and research, the occult content is quite apparent and sufficient to indicate an occult connection. If nothing else, the evidence would at least indicate that those who created the games or "those who researched and wrote the various manuals and materials . . . are well-versed in the occult."[19] It might also indicate something of far greater concern—something to which one researcher has referred in his summation: "After years of study of the history of occultism, after having researched a book on the topic, and after having consulted with scholars in the field of historical research, I can say with confidence: These games are the most effective, most magnificently packaged, most profitably marketed, most thoroughly researched introduction to the occult in man's recorded history."[20]

DANGERS OF OCCULTISM IN FRP GAMES

The world of the occult is by its own definition that which is immaterial, hidden, and esoteric. Webster defines occult as "hidden from the eye or understanding; invisible and mysterious . . ." or ". . . not revealed, secret; not easily apprehended

18. *San Diego Evening Tribune,* 13 October 1980.
19. Enroth, pp. 36-37.
20. Gary North, *Remnant Review,* 5 December 1980, p. 8.

or understood; not able to be seen or detected" Since the occult is by nature hidden from the eye and not able to be seen or detected, it would seem necessary for those who want to participate in the occult to use their imagination. Imagination, again according to Webster, is "the faculty by which we can bring absent objects and perceptions forcibly before the mind." It is "the act or power of forming a mental image of something not present to the senses or never before wholly perceived in reality." Imagination is the faculty by which one perceives and interacts with any reality not directly available through the five senses.

It is this potential relationship between the occult and the imagination that is of concern to many, especially in light of the obvious occult content in FRP games. As one researcher has noted:

> The very nature of D & D, and FRP in general, is such that the imagination is being guided into encounters with nonmaterial entities, forces, or spirits. Those entities, we are told, are mere fantasies with no basis in reality. If, however, those entities do actually exist in some form in the spirit world, then the line of demarcation between what is pure fantasy and what is actual contact with spiritual, demonic forces becomes extremely abstruse if not entirely nonexistent.[21]

This is not to say that there is no difference between actual participation in occult activities and imagining the same, or that every time someone participates in imaginative occult activity one is in contact with demonic forces. We simply point out that relegating "occult contact" to mere imagination does not guarantee one freedom from demonic influence.

Today, classes in psychic and spiritual development use imagination and visualization techniques in their methodolo-

---

21. Stanley Dokupil, *Dungeons and Dragons* (Berkeley, Calif.: Spiritual Counterfeits Project, 1982), pp. 3-4.

gy to achieve out-of-body experiences, develop occult powers, and foster contact with spirits. Many of the most popular books on various occult themes allude to these same techniques. Whether one likes to accept the fact or not, simple imagination has been used to establish spiritistic contact (e.g., when an imaginary counselor suddenly becomes a real being). There are numerous cases in occult literature where demons have actively sought out human contacts because of their "imagined" patron god, ascended master, counselor, or spirit helper.

Regardless of the difference between reality and imagination, a word of caution such as the following by Elliot Miller is necessary:

> However real this distinction may be in the minds of the players, though, I feel no assurance that the spirit world will not respond when it is beckoned.
>
> When I was of high-school age I was extremely skeptical about anything reputedly supernatural. I recall engaging in a mock seance with a group of friends. Our lightheartedness was turned to fear when suddenly the "medium," my best friend, began to convulse, his eyes rolled back in his head, and a strange voice emerged from his throat. For the following two years this young Jew was tormented by spirits. Withdrawing from all social contacts, he haunted graveyards until he was delivered through the power of Jesus Christ.[22]

Furthermore, there is always the possibility that a player may in everyday life pursue those occult activities role-played in fantasy. After all, the hope of every dreamer is to live the fantasy.

That some have pursued the occult as a result of their involvement in FRP games is a matter of record. On a major network radio talk show a few years ago, one prominent dun-

---

22. Brian Onken and Elliot Miller, "Dungeons and Dragons," *Forward* 4, no. 2:10.

geon master admitted to one of the authors that he personally knew of several who had gone on to become involved in witchcraft and spiritism as a result of playing D & D, but he was quick to point out that he saw no harm or danger in this. Subsequent dialogue revealed that his world view did not allow for anything supernatural. Thus, from his perspective, if there is no supernatural activity, then all occult activity must be understood in terms of the natural or paranormal. Participation in the occult cannot be (supernaturally) dangerous. We believe the world of demons is real, and that participation in the occult can be very dangerous.*

There is a supernatural world, which is real; a world in which not only God and His angels exist but also Satan and his demons. Many today doubt the existence of a real Satan or real demons. Yet if one were to honestly consider the positive consensus of history and religion—the testimony of active occultists as to the reality of evil spirits, the documented cases of demon possession, the hostility to historic biblical Christianity displayed in almost all spiritistically inspired literature, and the claims of the Bible and the testimony of Jesus Christ as to the reality of Satan and demons—one would find it difficult to deny their existence and involvement in our world. In light of the vast amount of evidence, to reject the possibility of the existence of Satan and demons solely on the basis of rationalistic or materialistic presuppositions would at best be foolish and at worst very dangerous.

In the Bible, God not only tells us of the dangers of Satan and demons but repeatedly warns us not to become involved in any way with the occult. When Israel was about to enter the land of Canaan, for example, God was very specific in naming the various practices and practitioners associated with the occult that they were to avoid.

---

*See John Weldon's *Hazards of Psychic Involvement: A Look at Some Consequences.* South Plainfield, N.J.: Bridge Publishers (forthcoming).

> When you enter the land which the Lord your God gives you,
> you shall not learn to imitate the detestable things of those
> nations. There shall not be found among you anyone who
> makes his son or his daughter pass through the fire, one who
> uses divination, one who practices witchcraft, or one who inter-
> prets omens, or a sorcerer, or one who casts a spell, or a
> medium, or a spiritist, or one who calls up the dead. For whoev-
> er does these things is detestable to the Lord. (Deuteronomy
> 18:9-12)

Throughout the years, Israel was not always faithful in
keeping God's word and rejecting the occult. King Saul
sought out a spiritistic medium at Endor in an attempt
to communicate with the prophet Samuel, who had died (see
1 Samuel 28:7-19). As a result of this act of disobedience
God "killed him, and turned the kingdom to David the son of
Jesse" (1 Chronicles 10:13-14).

On another occasion, King Manasseh disobeyed God and
pursued the occult. The list of charges against him are very
specific:

> He made his sons pass through the fire in the valley of Ben-
> hinnom; and he practiced witchcraft, used divination, practiced
> sorcery, and dealt with mediums and spiritists. He did much evil
> in the sight of the Lord, provoking Him to anger. (2 Chronicles
> 33:6)

God's method of punishing Manasseh and Israel for their
disobedience was to cause their defeat at the hands of the
Assyrian army. Manasseh himself was "captured . . . with
hooks, bound . . . with bronze chains, and (taken) to Babylon"
(2 Chronicles 33:11). While in captivity there, he humbled
himself before God and repented. When he was allowed to
return to the land, he undid much of the evil he had done
previously.

It should be obvious from the above that if God declares

that occult activity is wrong and expressly forbids involvement in it, then when a person participates he is disobeying
God. He should expect that God will not be pleased and that
that will have some negative spiritual impact on his life. In
addition, he should realize that by pursuing the occult, he
has opened himself up to the consequences associated with
such involvement (for Christians, potential manipulation by
demons and perhaps even the destruction of one's life; for
non-Christians, potential manipulation and possession by
demons—see Matthew 17:14-18 and Mark 5:1-15 for examples—and perhaps even the destruction of one's life).

One might argue that the only occult activity and involvement one pursues in FRP games is in fantasy. We know that
God forbids involvement in the occult in reality, but what
about in fantasy? How does God view someone's imaginative
involvement in the occult? As indicated earlier, if Jesus considered one's lusting after a woman *in his heart* (i.e., fantasy)
tantamount to adultery, what would He say about someone's
pursuing the occult *in his mind* (i.e., fantasy)? Would He approve, or would He say it was tantamount to occult participation? If one's mind is centered upon the "imaginative" use of
occult power, is he not at least tolerating the *idea* of its use?
And who can guarantee that the demonic will not respond?
Some players have reported actual paranormal or supernatural experiences (the movement of objects and other phe-
nomena) while playing these games.

We are admonished in the Bible to "be on the alert. Your
adversary, the devil, prowls about like a roaring lion, seeking
someone to devour" (1 Peter 5:8). We are also told that Satan
and his demons are master deceivers: "Satan disguises himself as an angel of light," and "his servants also disguise
themselves as servants of righteousness" (2 Corinthians
11:14-15). Satan can make something look desirable and
provide fun and excitement—he can use a game that encour-
ages fantasy and role playing—if it will attract someone to

become involved with him. We need to practice discernment continually "in order that no advantage be taken of us by Satan; for we are not ignorant of his schemes" (2 Corinthians 2:11).

Conclusion

Conclusion

No assessment of fantasy role-playing (FRP) games would be complete without at least some consideration of the claims made on their behalf as to their value.

First of all, advocates of FRP games claim that these games provide fun, excitement, and an opportunity to use one's imagination and enjoy fantasy. Any survey of players would certainly reveal that this has been the experience of many (though some have reported that they found playing to be "boring").

While FRP games advocates focus on the fun, excitement, and fantasy of these games, they seem to ignore or at least relegate to unimportance the context in which the fun and excitement takes place and the imagination is used. Yet it is this very context (and its content) that can make the difference between wholesome and not-so-wholesome fun, a good and evil use of fantasy, positive and negative influences on everyday life.

Second, advocates of FRP games have, for a long time, maintained that such games as Dungeons and Dragons® are harmless excursions into the world of fantasy and imagination and have a positive effect on the lives of their players.

That Dungeons and Dragons® is harmless and makes some positive contribution to the lives of its participants has been hotly contested, especially in the past few years. Both secular and religious observers have criticized the game for its occult overtones, its violence, and its potential for negatively affecting the lives of its players. Publicity in the media regarding alleged game-related suicides and other problems has only created further doubt as to the harmless nature and positive effects of Dungeons and Dragons®.

All of this has not gone unnoticed by TSR Hobbies, Inc. (the manufacturer). A few years ago they began to mount something of a public relations campaign to counter this "bad press." In an effort to reassure the public (and particularly the religious sector) that Dungeons and Dragons® is harmless and that it really has a positive impact on the lives of its players, TSR published the following announcement in its monthly periodical, *The Dragon:*

> If you are a player of D & D or AD & D who is also a member of
> the clergy of any organized religion—or a lay person who knows
> of such an individual—you can be of great help to TSR Hobbies,
> Inc. TSR Hobbies is seeking opinions and observations about
> the games from members of the clergy who are players or Dun-
> geon Masters, or from men and women who have careers in or
> associated with religion and possess firsthand knowledge of the
> game's helpful, positive influence on those who play it.[1]

No one but TSR Hobbies, Inc., knows the number of responses they actually received. The only known responses are the two they have included in their "media kit." The first, "A Minister Responds," is by the Reverend Escoe L. Robinson III, an ordained minister and graduate of Atlanta Christian

---

1. "Real Life Clerics: TSR Needs You," *The Dragon,* August 1980, p. 49.

College. He attempts to answer several criticisms regarding the AD & D game. The second, "Reflections of a Real-life Cleric," is by the Reverend Arthur W. Collins, an ordained minister in the United Methodist Church. He seeks to extol the virtues and uses of fantasy and of role playing.

If, as fantasy role-playing game advocates claim, such games as D & D are indeed harmless and have made a positive contribution to the lives of players, it seems that the burden of proof lies with them (especially since there appears to be evidence to the contrary). Thus far very little in the way of evidence has been produced to substantiate their claim.

Third, advocates of FRP games assert that the games provide special educational qualities and opportunity. Usually they mention the fact that Dungeons and Dragons® has been used throughout the United States in a number of programs for the gifted and talented, which is true.

Some educators have indicated their support for this claim by pointing out that Dungeons and Dragons® develops and reinforces important skills such as reading, listening, mathematical computation, mapping, logical reasoning, and so on. There is no doubt that players must read the game's rules system and ancillary materials, listen to verbal instructions, use various tables for computation, employ mapping skills in creating the fantasy milieu (as dungeon master), reason logically in playing the game, or do research in the library when necessary, nor is there any doubt that there is some value in this. But, as other educators have noted, there are many other ways to develop and reinforce the very same skills, and more.

Others have indicated their support by pointing out that such games develop and reinforce cooperation among the players. Obviously, players must work together in the game, but again, cooperation can be developed in many other ways as well. It should be noted here that a few educators have indicated their concern over a distorted development of this "cooperation." In some cases, players have formed cliques that have spilled over into everyday life and have not been confined just to point-gathering during game time.

The greatest educational value of Dungeons and Dragons®, according to approving educators, lies in its ability to stimulate and develop creativity. There has been some debate as to the value of such creativity, however. One researcher has stated: "To date, however, little evidence exists that D & D players are being creatively stimulated to do anything other than to continue to play D & D."[2] Thus, to conclude, as many FRP advocates have done, that these games have great or special educational value would require much more research and favorable evidence than is presently available.

The above are three of the claims made by advocates of FRP games. There may be others that need consideration and response, but these essentially represent the major claims made today.

Although no assessment of FRP games would be complete without at least some consideration of these claims, it should also be noted that no assessment should be limited only to a consideration of those claims. A careful examination and evaluation of FRP games in the areas of those categories discussed in chapters 4 and 5 (i.e., the role of fantasy, morality, escapism, and the occult) is absolutely necessary if one is going to honestly and objectively assess whether or not he should participate in these games.

Fantasy. We have already seen that our ability to fantasize is God-given. There is a good use of fantasy but also an evil use. Fantasy role-playing games in general seem to promote the wrong use of fantasy by presenting character roles that assume power, violence, immorality, and sorcery—all things God hates. Furthermore, such role playing could affect the lives of players, especially those pre-adolescent and adoles-

---

2. Stanley Dokupil, *Dungeons and Dragons* (Berkeley, Calif.: Spiritual Counterfeits Project, 1982), p. 2.

cent players who are still in the formative stages of developing their personal philosophy, world view, moral system, and self-image.

Morality. FRP games in general present and promote at best an amoral universe. Since this universe appears to be essentially non-theistic, it can be non-supportive of any God-given morality. In fact, the games contain many activities and practices that God forbids and condemns in the Bible. Thus FRP games have the potential to undermine or negate the influence of Christian morality in any player's life.

Escape. Escape, when connected with fantasy, is part of God's creation. Like fantasy, it can be used in a wholesome and healthy way or it can be misused. The complexity and ego involvement in fantasy role-playing games in general appear to provide the potential for an unhealthy use of escape and a wasting of valuable time.

Occult. We have seen that FRP games in general seem to present and promote the occult. These games are not as sinister as the Ouija board, which is actually designed for spiritistic contact, but neither are they as harmless as Monopoly®. The occult content in what appears to be a glorification of the occult as a tool for creative fantasy has the potential to lead to occult involvement. It simply is not wise to participate in these games. There is always the danger of actual contact with the powers of darkness.

It is obvious from our assessment that there are a number of questionable areas and potential problems (and dangers) associated with current fantasy role-playing games, such as Dungeons and Dragons®. Collectively, these problems should provide sufficient reason for one to avoid any involvement with these games. They should cause one to think twice about participation or to reconsider any already existing involvement.

The final decision as to whether or not you should participate in such games is yours to make before God in light of your own personal assessment.

Examine everything carefully; hold fast to that which is good; abstain from every form of evil.

And may the God of Peace Himself sanctify you entirely; and may your spirit and soul and body be preserved complete, without blame at the coming of our Lord Jesus Christ. (1 Thessalonians 5:21-23)

Selected Bibliography

Selected Bibliography

Books

Gygax, Gary. *Dungeons and Dragons* (basic manual). Lake Geneva, Wis.: TSR Hobbies, 1979.

———. *Dungeons and Dragons Players Handbook.* Lake Geneva, Wis.: TSR Games, 1975.

———. *Advanced Dungeons and Dragons Players Handbook.* Lake Geneva, Wis.: TSR Games, 1978.

Holmes, John E. *Fantasy Role Playing Games.* New York: Hippocrene, 1981.

Kuntz, Robert, and Ward, James. *Gods, Demigods, and Heroes.* Lake Geneva, Wis.: TSR Games, 1976.

Ward, James M., and Kuntz, Robert J. *Deities and Demigods: Cyclopedia of Gods and Heroes from Myth and Legend,* ed. Lawrence Schick. Lake Geneva, Wis.: TSR Games, 1980.

Periodicals

The Best of the Dragon. (TSR Periodicals, Lake Geneva, WI 53147.)

Dager, Albert J. "Dungeons and Dragons, A Media Spotlight Special Report," *Media Spotlight: A Christian Review of Entertainment.* 3, no. 2. (*Media Spotlight,* 1102 E. Chestnut Ave., Santa Ana, CA 92071.)

Dokupil, Stanley. *Dungeons and Dragons: Fantasy Role Playing and the Occult.* 1982. (Spiritual Counterfeits Project, P.O. Box 4308, Berkeley, CA 94704.)

Dragon. (Dragon Publishing, Lake Geneva, WI 53147.)

Dungeons and Dragons: Only a Game? (Pro Family Forum, P.O. Box 8907, Fort Worth, TX 76112.)

Enroth, Ronald M. "Fantasy Games: Is There an Occult Connection?" *Eternity,* December 1981.

Hewson, Martha. "A Game That Casts a Spell," *McCalls,* October 1980.

Holmes, John E. "Confessions of a Dungeon Master," *Psychology Today,* November 1980.

Johnston, Moira. "It's Only a Game—Or Is It?" *New West,* 25, August, 1980.

MacRae, Paul. "The Art of War for Fun and Profit," *MacLeans,* 21 April 1980.

Onken, Brian, and Miller, Elliot. "Dungeons and Dragons," *Forward* 4, no. 2. (Christian Research Institute, 22672 Lambert Street, Suite 604, El Toro, CA 92603.)

Smith, Geoffrey. "Dungeons and Dollars," *Forbes,* 15 September 1980.

Ten Elshof, Phyllis. "Dungeons and Dragons: A Fantasy Fad, or Dabbling in the Demonic?" *Christianity Today,* 4 September and 2 October 1981.

Williams, Katherine. "Dungeons and Dragons," *Cornerstone,* 9, no. 52. (Jesus People USA, 4431 N. Paulina, Chicago, IL 60640.)

NEWSPAPERS

Christian Science Monitor, 9 February and 18 March 1981.
Courier & Press (Evansville, Ind.), 21 February 1982.

Florida Times-Union (Jacksonville, Fla.), 2 August 1981.
Los Angeles Times, 24, 25, 26 June and 12 December 1981.
Manchester (N.H.) Union Leader, 17 August 1980.
New York Times, 30 May 1980.
Orange County (Calif.) *Register,* 17 May 1981.
Sacramento Bee, 12 June 1981.
San Diego Evening Tribune, 13 October 1980.
Seattle Times, 21 October 1981.
The Sunday Record (Bergen County, N.J.), 8 March 1981.
Washington Post, 27 June 1980.